GHOST STORIES

GHOSTS AT SEA

By Lisa Owings

EPIC

BELLWETHER MEDIA • MINNEAPOLIS, MN

EPIC BOOKS are no ordinary books. They burst with intense action, high-speed heroics, and shadows of the unknown. Are you ready for an Epic adventure?

This edition first published in 2017 by Bellwether Media, Inc.

No part of this publication may be reproduced in whole or in part without written permission of the publisher.
For information regarding permission, write to Bellwether Media, Inc., Attention: Permissions Department,
5357 Penn Avenue South, Minneapolis, MN 55419.

Library of Congress Cataloging-in-Publication Data

Names: Owings, Lisa, author.
Title: Ghosts at Sea / by Lisa Owings.
Description: Minneapolis, MN : Bellwether Media Inc., 2017. | Series: Epic:
   Ghost Stories | Includes bibliographical references and index.
Identifiers: LCCN 2015045392 | ISBN 9781626174252 (hardcover : alk. paper)
Subjects: LCSH: Ghosts–Juvenile literature. | Ocean–Folklore.
Classification: LCC BF1486 .O95 2017 | DDC 133.1/22–dc23
LC record available at http://lccn.loc.gov/2015045392

Printed in the United States of America, North Mankato, MN.

TABLE OF CONTENTS

SPOOKY SEAS

Black waves stretch to no end. Clouds mask the moon. Far off, a ship appears in **eerie** light. Are there ghosts aboard?

Sailors often tell stories of ghosts at sea. **Cursed** ships and **crews** haunt their tales.

THE CURSED CREW

One story tells of the *Flying Dutchman*. Dutch captain Van der Decken sailed this ship long ago.

HISTORY CONNECTION

Composer Richard Wagner made the *Flying Dutchman* famous. In 1840, he wrote an opera about the ship.

His crew was rounding Africa's **Cape** of Good Hope. As they neared the rocks, the sky went dark. Wind tore at the sails. Waves beat against the ship.

Cape of
Good Hope

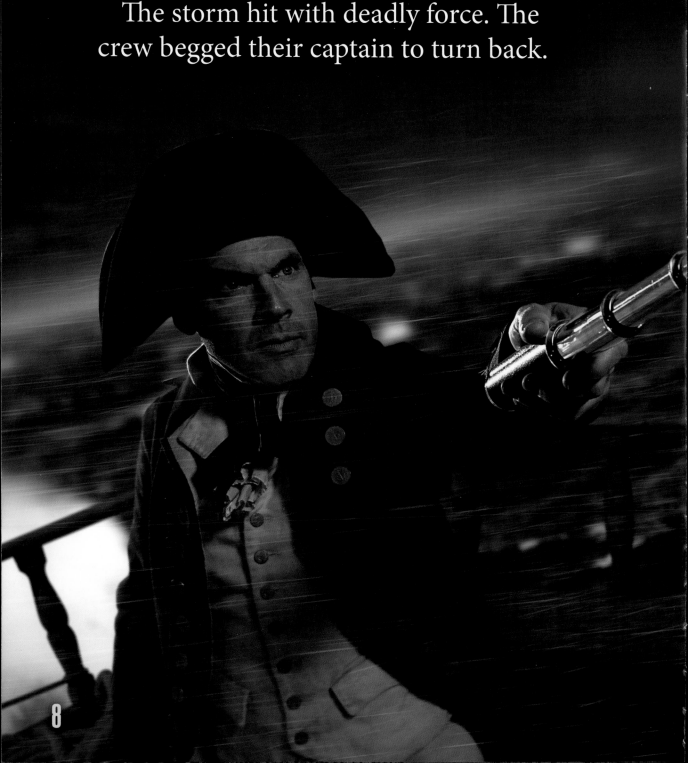

The storm hit with deadly force. The crew begged their captain to turn back.

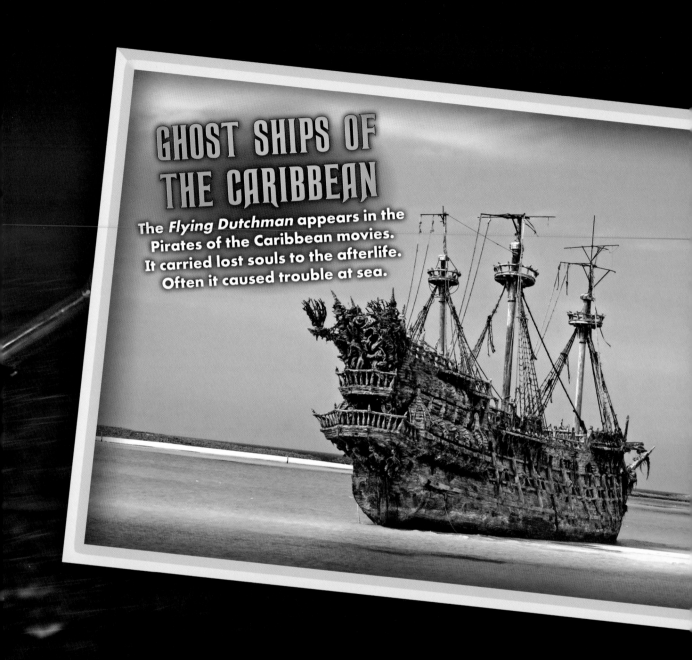

GHOST SHIPS OF THE CARIBBEAN

The *Flying Dutchman* appears in the Pirates of the Caribbean movies. It carried lost souls to the afterlife. Often it caused trouble at sea.

Van der Decken ignored them. He swore he would round the cape. Even if he had to sail forever!

TALL TALES

There are many versions of this story. Some claim true love will lift the captain's curse. Others say the ghostly crew leaves letters for loved ones on passing ships.

Churning waves swallowed captain and crew. But they never found rest. The captain's foolish promise **doomed** them to sail forever.

The **phantom** ship sails in stormy weather. Many claim to have seen it. For some, bad luck follows.

SIGHTINGS OF THE FLYING DUTCHMAN

- British sailors claim a ghost ship nearly crashed into them (1835)

- The future King George V of Britain records his ship's encounter with a glowing ship (1881)

- Ship races toward South African shore, then disappears (1939)

- German submarine crews claim to see ghost ship (1942)

One crewman decided capture would be worse than death. So he threw a torch into a barrel of gunpowder.

The *Young Teazer* exploded in a fiery blaze. Few survived the flames.

THE TEAZER LIGHT

Locals call this flaming ship the Teazer Light. They look for it on June 27. That is the date of the ship's ruin.

A ghostly *Young Teazer* still haunts Mahone Bay. Some moonlit nights, a burning ship appears. The screams of its crew fill the air. Then the ship disappears.

SIGHTINGS OF THE YOUNG TEAZER

- Seen on foggy nights on the date of its sinking

- Sank in front of watchers at Borgal's Point

- Ghostly crew sighted as the *Young Teazer* nearly ran down a boat near Clam Island

- Last sighting reported in 1935

JUST STORIES?

Skeptics believe science explains ghost ship sightings. They say the ships are **fata morganas**. These **mirages** have strange effects. They can make objects seem to float. Some form mirror images.

ALIENS AHOY?

Fata morganas have fooled many. They explain some UFO sightings.

A full moon behind fog can look like a burning ship. But can this explain empty ships racing over waves? Or long-dead sailors on deck?

Some sea-loving spooks may be tricks of the eye. But many believe ghosts still haunt the seas.

GLOSSARY

cape—a rocky piece of land that sticks out into the water

crews—groups of people who work together on ships

cursed—under an evil spell

doomed—unable to escape an awful situation

eerie—strange and spooky

fata morganas—visions that are a type of mirage; fata morganas can make ships appear doubled or like they are floating.

mirages—things that look real but are not actually there; mirages are caused by hot air that bends light rays.

phantom—ghostly

pirates—people who attack and rob ships at sea; privateers are pirates who are hired by a country to attack enemy ships in times of war.

skeptics—people who doubt the truth of something

War of 1812—a war fought between the United States and Great Britain between 1812 and 1815

TO LEARN MORE

AT THE LIBRARY

Gould, Jane H. *The Flying Dutchman*. New York, N.Y.:
PowerKids Press, 2015.

Higgins, Nadia. *Ghosts*. Minneapolis, Minn.: Bellwether
Media, 2014.

Owings, Lisa. *Ghost Ships*. Minneapolis, Minn.: Bellwether
Media, 2015.

ON THE WEB

Learning more about
ghosts at sea is
as easy as 1, 2, 3.

1. Go to www.factsurfer.com.

2. Enter "ghosts at sea" into the search box.

3. Click the "Surf" button and you will see a list
   of related web sites.

With factsurfer.com, finding more information
is just a click away.

INDEX

The images in this book are reproduced through the courtesy of: Philip Willcocks, front cover (ghost), p. 20 (ghost); cdrin, front cover (ship), pp. 1, 20 (ship); Ryszard Filipowicz, pp. 4-5 (ship); DMG Vision, pp. 4-5 (background); John Lund/ Blend Images/ SuperStock, pp. 6-7; Jay P. Morgan/ Exactostock-1598/ SuperStock, p. 8; Lucy Clark, p. 9; Andrey Yurlov, pp. 10-11 (background); Howard Oates, pp. 10-11 (ship); David Turnley/ Corbis, p. 13; BoringRed, p. 14; Nadezhda Bolotina, p. 15 (ship); John Panella, p. 15 (explosion); Nils Prause, p. 16 (ship); L Lazuma, p. 16 (background); Durk Talsma, p. 16 (flames); Istimages, p. 19 (background); Kate Sfeir, p. 19 (ship); die Fotosynthese, p. 21 (ship); Jakob Fischer, p. 21 (background).